JOHN WAIN

FRANK

AMBER LANE PRESS

All rights whatsoever in this play are strictly reserved and
application for performance, etc. should be made before
rehearsal to:

Curtis Brown Limited,
162–168 Regent Street,
London W1R 5TA.

No performance may be given unless a licence has been
obtained.

First published in 1984 by
Amber Lane Press Ltd,
9 Middle Way, Oxford OX2 7LH

Typeset by Midas Publishing Services, Ltd, Oxford

Printed in Great Britain by
Cotswold Press Ltd, Oxford

ISBN 0 906399 55 6

Frank was first broadcast by the BBC on Monday 4th October 1982. The recording was directed by Jane Morgan and the cast was as follows:

FRANK	Tony Osoba
FRANK (as a child)/SAM	Susan Sheridan
DR LEVET	Peter Vaughan
MISS ANNA WILLIAMS	Sian Phillips
BETSY	Jill Lidstone
DR WRIGHT	Hugh Dickson
SISTER	Katherine Parr
COLONEL BATHURST	Jack May
RICHARD BATHURST	David Banks
ABIGAIL	Kathryn Hurlbutt
CAPTAIN	Roger Allam
PLANTATION OWNER/ DOCTOR JOHNSON	Michael Graham Cox

FOREWORD

THIS PLAY is an exercise of the imagination, an attempt to breathe life into a sparse handful of dry facts. Sparse in one way, abundant in another. At the centre of the source-material is a baffling dearth of information. All around it is a coruscating fountain, an overplus.

It is not my intention to talk in riddles. Frank Barber entered Samuel Johnson's household as a boy of about seven (his date of birth is unknown) in 1752. Apart from two periods of truancy, which we will come to in a moment, he never left that household. It left him, thirty-two years later, when Johnson died. By that time, Johnson appears to have accepted Frank in the role of a son. He had evolved to that role through others, and had been a long time on the road. But when he came to make his will, Johnson accepted the responsibility to provide for Frank, as he had accepted it since the first day they met. Apart from a few particular presents to friends — a book here, an item of furniture there — he left Frank everything. It was enough to make a future for Frank, for his wife Betsy, for their children. They came close to being Johnson's own family. Certainly they were his relicts.

To write a play about this situation is to encounter the two conditions I mentioned at the beginning. About Johnson we have a rich harvest of information — owing, in the first place, to the devotion of his friends, notably James Boswell, and in the second place to the dedication of five generations of scholars, beginning with Boswell's own contemporary, Edmund Malone. This information also reaches out to the strange household that Johnson maintained, the various misfits and casualties of life who drifted towards him and found a haven below stairs in his house in Gough Square, off Fleet Street. We know a great deal in one way and another about Anna Williams, the daughter of a Welsh physician; she became totally blind after an unsuccessful operation for cataract. She had been a friend of Johnson's wife Elizabeth

('Tetty'), and Johnson as a widower had kept her friendship
and enjoyed it, for she was an intelligent, well-read woman.
Johnson advised her to have the operation, and after its
failure he had taken on the responsibility of seeing that she
had a roof over her head. We know something, too, about
Robert Levet, the gruff old Yorkshireman who, without pro-
fessional training except what he had picked up by hanging
around Paris hospitals during the years when he had worked
in that city as a waiter, practised the healing art among the
poorest of the poor, and was a trusted confidant of Johnson —
so justifiably trusted that he took Johnson's secrets to the
grave with him. And about others whom I screened out of the
play, not because they were not there in the household but
because the list of characters was becoming, for a seventy-five-
minute radio play, unmanageably long and indigestibly rich:
Mrs Desmoulins, daughter of Johnson's godfather Dr Swin-
fen, who had married a French Huguenot writing-master
and, when widowed, came to Johnson's household, where she
quarrelled incessantly with Anna Williams; and Poll Car-
michael, who seems to have had a previous career as a girl of
the London pavements. Johnson, with his great heart and his
always open purse, sheltered these people and looked after
them because, as he sensibly remarked, no one else would
have done and what would they do then?

Frank, by many years the youngest member of this circle,
evidently looked at it with a jaundiced eye. In the earlier part
of his life he made two attempts to escape. The first was when
he ran away and took a job with an apothecary in Cheapside.
The charm of mixing ointments and grinding powders did
not last long and he was soon back home. The second attempt
was more ambitious. Frank joined the Navy and was in it for
two years. This, the most extraordinary episode in his life, is
also the least documented. If anyone took the trouble to ask
him, when he got back, what his motives had been, and how he
felt about Johnson's action in procuring his discharge, they
did not take the further trouble of writing down what Frank
said. His motives for that astonishing action (and astonishing

it must always remain, when we remember what life in the 18th-century Navy was like), must be, like his thoughts and feelings generally, a matter of conjecture.

Nevertheless, the conjecture has to be made if we are to think of Frank Barber at all. He was a human being, he lived in this world for over half a century, he fell in love and married and reared a family; and he was the personal servant of one of the greatest Englishmen. Johnson's attitude to Frank was compassionate and considerate. Hating the slave trade, hating the thought of the abject condition of life into which Frank had been born, he was always careful not to tread on Frank's feelings. When their cat needed fish — generally oysters, which were very cheap in those days — Johnson, the famous sage and scholar, Johnson with his royal pension, Johnson who was admired by the most brilliant men and women of his age, would go out personally on this humble errand, lest Frank should feel himself degraded by having to attend on an animal.

That delicacy characterized Johnson's attitude to Frank. Of Frank's attitude to Johnson we have no direct knowledge. We can only infer and conjecture. Of such inferences and conjectures is this play fashioned. It seemed a subject worth attempting.

John Wain, January 1984

1. Stafford Infirmary: a night in January, 1801. A bell is ringing.

DR WRIGHT: Well, Sister... [*He exhales loudly as he sinks into his chair.*] That's the worst day of the month over, thank the Lord.

SISTER: Yes, Doctor. You always do find these Tuesday visits try your patience.

DR WRIGHT: We must be charitable, Sister, at least I suppose we must. The Scriptures enjoin it. But why the Committee of Management of Stafford Infirmary, a pack of well-meaning meddlers with too much time on their hands and not a particle of scientific knowledge in their heads, should descend on me on the first Tuesday afternoon of every month, poking into this and that, looking into accounts they don't understand, dawdling about in the wards and getting in the way of essential work — and then go home late in the evening with a self-satisfied feeling that they've done something for humanity... it defeats me. I just don't understand it.

SISTER: Excuse me, Dr Wright. I thought I heard a knock at the door.

DR WRIGHT: A knock? At the door of my private study, where I am never to be disturbed? Has this hospital no discipline, Sister? Has it no organisation?

> [SISTER *goes to the door and opens it, while* DR WRIGHT *in foreground groans wearily.*]

> [*The following dialogue is heard in the background.*]

SISTER: The Doctor isn't seeing anyone.

BETSY: But it's only for a moment.

SISTER: This is his private study.

BETSY: Just one question.

SISTER: He's not giving consultations, come on Thursday morning.

BETSY: Just one minute for one question! I have to know! It's important!

> [BETSY *pushes the* SISTER *aside and rushes into the room.*]

SISTER: [*despairingly*] This lady, sir — she won't take no for an answer! I don't know how she got in...

BETSY: [*advancing*] Dr Wright, how is my husband?

DR WRIGHT: My good woman, you simply cannot force your way into a hospital, into the private study of the superintendent of a hospital, late in the evening, and start firing off questions about an individual patient.

BETSY: I've a right to know how he is, Doctor. This isn't an ordinary patient like your village people from round here. This is an important person, this is Mr Francis Barber!

DR WRIGHT: And you, I take it, madam, are Mrs Barker.

BETSY: Barber, Barber, don't you know who I'm talking about?

SISTER: [*interposes aside*] The black man, sir.

BETSY: He's not just any old black man, he's the Francis Barber who was manservant to Dr Johnson for thirty years!

DR WRIGHT: Well, madam, what is it you want to know?

BETSY: I brought him in two nights ago with a bad fever. Since then I haven't heard a word about how he is, and I'm not going away till I do.

DR WRIGHT: Well, Sister, since this lady is clearly in no mood to listen to reason, I suppose the simplest way of getting rid of her would be to answer her question. Since every fourth Tuesday is my day for being pestered by the Committee of Management, I had no time to walk through the wards this evening, but you must have done. What condition is this Mr Barber in?

SISTER: His condition is unchanged, sir. He has a tertian fever.

DR WRIGHT: Yes, yes, I diagnosed it myself, you will recall. Well, Mrs Barber, you have your answer: your husband's fever is still unabated. You will have to be patient.

BETSY: But what are you doing for him?

DR WRIGHT: Doing for him? He has soothing potions, he has rest, quiet and warmth. There is nothing more that any human power can do for him. And now, madam, if you will kindly take your leave...

[SISTER *leads* BETSY *towards the door.*]

SISTER: Come along now, dear.

BETSY: Can I see him? I've been waiting all day.

SISTER: No visitors in the wards, dear, until Thursday afternoon. Come along now, we'll do everything to look after
him.

[SISTER *ushers* BETSY *out and closes the door.*]

SISTER: She's gone, Doctor. Sorry you were bothered. She was
half out of her mind with worry, sir. We get them like
that all the time.

DR WRIGHT: Worry doesn't give her the right to come pushing
in here. If these women want to keep their husbands
where they can see them all the time, they should let
them stay at home to die. I suppose he is dying, by the
way?

SISTER: Yes, sir. I've given him a sleeping-draught to stop him
making too much noise and disturbing the other
patients, but I doubt if he'll last the night.

DR WRIGHT: Well, by tomorrow morning I expect he'll be the
late Francis Barber, who was an important person.
These people certainly have more than their share of
local pride. [*in mock tones of awe*] He was Dr Johnson's
servant. For thirty years! And who might Dr Johnson
have been? Some benevolent family physician, I suppose, from Lichfield or Uttoxeter, not above taking a
look at a sick cow or horse as well as a sick human being.
I honour such a man. But he can't have been eminent in
the medical profession, or I'd have heard of him... This
sleeping-draught you gave him, Sister, it was a good
strong one, I hope?

SISTER: The strongest, sir. And I made him finish it.

DR WRIGHT: Well, with any luck he should pass away fairly
peacefully. The few hours that are left to him will be
mostly dreams, and I hope for his sake that they're
pleasant ones.

2. Sea and ship noises and FRANK's *feverish breathing.*

VOICES: Barber to report to the captain — Barber to report to the captain [*echoing*] the captain, the captain.

FRANK: [*feverish voice*] It's always the same. It's always report to the captain and then he tells me my discharge has come. I've got to leave the ship.

Captain, do I have to go? My discharge? — I don't want no discharge. I like this ship, sir, I'm happy under your command, sir, you've always been a good captain to me, do I have to go?

VOICE OF ROBERT LEVET: Yes, lad, the answer's yes.

FRANK: Dr Levet! What are you doing on this ship?

LEVET: I'm not on a ship, lad, and neither are you. I don't know where your mind's wandering to, but you're right about one thing — you've got your discharge and you're going.

FRANK: Going? Where to?

LEVET: Oh, just to the ghosts' clearing-house. The dead place.

FRANK: But I'm alive! I don't want to be dead!

LEVET: It's nothing to worry about, lad. Being dead's all right. It's even quite pleasant. You can put on a ghost's outfit and walk about and watch everybody at it, with no worries of your own. You're above it all, see. Or... to one side of it, like.

FRANK: Uh-uh. I don't want to be dead.

LEVET: Look, I'm dead, Dr Johnson's dead, Miss Williams is dead, there's nothing to it. Before this night's out you'll be dead and then you'll see.

FRANK: I might get better. If my head would just cool off and go down to normal size, I might get better.

LEVET: No, you won't.

FRANK: Why are you so sure?

LEVET: Because you can hear me. Only people who are already half in the next world can hear what a ghost says. And leaving aside a few odd cases, poets and prophets and such, for most people that means when they're just about to die. Half-way through the fence already, see?

[*An insistent, single-note bell is heard.*]

FRANK: I can't die. I have to get out in the field. Hear the bell? When that bell rings, all the slaves have to get out in the field and start picking the cotton. If the overseer comes and finds you still in your hut, boy, he'll flog you till the flies'll buzz round that blood on your back. I can't die — I've got to get out there!

LEVET: Get off. It's fifty years since you worked in the plantation. All that happened when you were a child.

FRANK: [*his voice at five years old*] But I am a child. My mammy said to do what the overseer he told me, then he wouldn't whip me so hard. I'm going out there.

[*The bell ceases.*]

JOHNSON'S VOICE: Frank!

LEVET: There you are. It's not the overseer who wants you, it's the Doctor. You'd better go to him.

FRANK: [*adult voice*] What does he want now? I took him his breakfast earlier on.

LEVET: That was an hour ago. Why shouldn't he want you? You're his servant, aren't you?

FRANK: So they say. I never wanted to be his servant.

LEVET: You don't have to do much.

FRANK: [*aside*] Trust a white man to talk like that. He gets free board and lodging here and what does he do?

LEVET: I heard that, lad. I know you didn't say it out loud, but a ghost can tell what people are thinking.

FRANK: All right, that's what I'm thinking.

LEVET: That just shows you don't understand. The truth is, it all falls on me.

FRANK: What all falls on you?

LEVET: The job of understanding the Doctor.

JOHNSON'S VOICE: Frank!

LEVET: You'd better go to him.

FRANK: How can I if I'm dying?

LEVET: Look, some people would say you were lying in Stafford Infirmary. But in your own mind, when I first came in here you were in the Navy. Then you were on the plantation. Well, now you just tell your mind you're in the kitchen in Dr Johnson's house in Gough Square. I tell you, when time starts dancing about, the only thing to do is dance with it.

FRANK: Oh, all right. [*calls*] I'm coming right up, Dr Johnson. [*He goes out.*]

LEVET: [*resumes his thread*] Understood the Doctor. I should say I did. And a good thing too. There wasn't nobody else. All the people pestering round him: there wasn't one that knew anything about what went on in his mind. Same with that Williams woman. Lived in his house all those years and never understood him. Blind in the body and blind in the spirit.

VOICE OF ANNA WILLIAMS: Are you under the impression, Robert Levet, that I can't hear you?

LEVET: Oh, godfathers.

ANNA WILLIAMS: And since I can hear you, are you under the impression that I will allow such slanders to pass unchallenged?

LEVET: I didn't know you could hear me, not that I'd have said anything different. The truth's the truth.

ANNA WILLIAMS: Lame excuses won't mend matters. You know that any remark made by a ghost can always be heard by any other ghost.

LEVET: Only if the other ghost happens to be in earshot. And you're not always around, snooping and eavesdropping.

ANNA WILLIAMS: No, I am not always around. I spend most of my time in Wales, as is natural for a Welsh ghost.

LEVET: Yes, go and pester that lot. They're used to it. Stay on the other side of Offa's Dyke and give us a bit of peace.

ANNA WILLIAMS: Peace! You don't know the meaning of the word. You're too cantankerous.

LEVET: Honest'd be a better word for it. I didn't dish out a lot of soft soap to every fool who came round to waste the Doctor's time.

ANNA WILLIAMS: Yes, the Doctor relied on me to keep up the tone of his household, to show courtesy to visitors.

LEVET: Leaving aside all the fancy talk, you spent your life pouring out tea, with your finger inside the rim of the cup to tell when it was getting near the top.

ANNA WILLIAMS: I am not ashamed of that. There is no other way a blind person can pour out tea. Dr Johnson always said I was a perfect hostess. But you wouldn't understand about that. I had the background of a lady, a woman of letters. My father, as I suppose I must once more remind you, was a qualified physician.

LEVET: Your father had a piece of paper to say he was a doctor. But pieces of paper don't make people well when they're ill and suffering. I've cured more sick people than your father had hot dinners — and they were only leek soup and pig's trotters.

[*Sound of opening door:* FRANK *is back.*]

FRANK: [*aside*] Quarrelling again, quarrelling year after year. Doesn't being a ghost change a person's nature at all?

ANNA WILLIAMS: [*to* LEVET] Instead of spending your energies in thinking up low insults, you would do better to try to set a worthy example to this unfortunate heathen child.

FRANK: [*aside*] That's typical. I wasn't a heathen. Colonel Bathurst had me christened and the Doctor taught me to say my prayers. And the plantation... didn't we sing hymns on the plantation? I seem to remember... But I was so little.

[*Sound of black voices singing a religious song.*]

FRANK: I wasn't a heathen. She just meant I had a black skin.

LEVET: Anna Williams. An old Welsh witch without a broomstick. The Doctor'd have been a lot better without you and your kind.

ANNA WILLIAMS: I don't know what you mean by my kind, but if you mean well-read cultivated ladies, the Doctor depended a good deal on their company.

LEVET: I never saw the man yet as wouldn't be better off without women.

ANNA WILLIAMS: It's a pity you didn't try to inculcate a little of that attitude into Frank. Till he met Betsy, who I agree was the salvation of him, he did nothing but get into scrapes with the girls.

FRANK: [*appreciatively*] Scrapes! They may have been scrapes at the time but they're good memories now.

LEVET: Not for me, they aren't. There were years when we never knew where the next upset was coming from. That time the Doctor took you down into Lincolnshire. I wonder you weren't ashamed to lead a country girl astray. She thought you were magic because you came from London.

FRANK: Abigail... She was lovely. So fresh and pink with all that country air. I told her I lived in a castle in London with a hundred other black men and we were all kings.

LEVET: She can't have believed that.

FRANK: She didn't, she just liked to be told stories. By the time I had to come away and leave her she didn't care where I lived.

LEVET: She may not have cared, but she knew, and what a scene she made, the little hell-cat.

ANNA WILLIAMS: I don't blame the girl. She was a simple country virgin who had been betrayed by this bad, thoughtless, heathen boy here.

LEVET: She was a hell-cat. You don't remember how bad it was.

[*Voice of Lincolnshire girl,* ABIGAIL, *heard, dream-like, as if shouting across a distance.*]

ABIGAIL: Frank! Frank! I'm here to rescue you! Jack's here with the wagon — you can come today!

FRANK: [*reminiscent*] I'll never forget when she turned up, in the middle of the morning.

LEVET: I'd be damn' glad to forget it.

ANNA WILLIAMS: A disgraceful scene — and in the Doctor's house too.

[*We now hear the scene in question. A knocking heard at the street door; footsteps going upstairs.*]

LEVET: Who's in such an almighty hurry?

[*The door opens.*]

ABIGAIL: Where's Frank?

LEVET: What's it to you?

ABIGAIL: Stand out of my way! I've come for Frank!

LEVET: [*calling down the stairs*] Frank! There's a wench here says she's come for you!

ABIGAIL: [*also calling downstairs*] It's me, Frank, Abigail! I've come to rescue you!

LEVET: What the devil d'you mean, rescue him?

ABIGAIL: Yes, I'm not surprised you swear by the devil. He's your master, isn't he?

LEVET: Is everybody going mad?

ABIGAIL: Frank told me he was going to send for me and I was going to come to London and be his wife.

LEVET: Oh, I see.

ABIGAIL: And I know why he didn't.

LEVET: Why didn't he?

ABIGAIL: Because of you. Because of the bad, wicked people there must be in this house. Either you're keeping him a prisoner here, or else you're what you look like, a wicked old magician who's put a spell on him to make him forget Abigail. Whichever it is, I'm here to rescue him!

LEVET: Go ahead, go ahead, rescue him. I'll not stand in your way.

[ABIGAIL's *footsteps are heard hurrying downstairs, bursting into the kitchen.*]

ABIGAIL: What — where's Frank?

ANNA WILLIAMS: I don't know who you are, my girl, but Frank was in here a moment ago, speaking to me. Is he not still here?

ABIGAIL: Where have you hidden him?

ANNA WILLIAMS: A blind person does not hide things, my girl, or people.

LEVET: [*entering*] I'm not going to miss this, Frank! Where are you? It's your sweetheart, the one you're going to marry!

ABIGAIL: Frank! Frank! I'm here to rescue you! Where have they hidden you?

LEVET: At a guess I'd say... try the cupboard.

[*The cupboard door is rattled.*]

ABIGAIL: It's locked.

LEVET: He's in there all right. There's nowhere else he could be.

ABIGAIL: Frank, it's Abigail! Have they locked you in the cupboard? Are you tied up?

[*Burst of rusty laughter from* LEVET.]

ANNA WILLIAMS: Can nothing quiet the unfortunate girl? The Doctor will hear her.

FRANK: [*through the door*] Abigail, go away.

ABIGAIL: Go away?

FRANK: I'm in this cupboard because I like it.

LEVET: I wouldn't have missed this for the world.

ABIGAIL: I'm here to rescue you, Frank! Jack's here with the wagon — we came up last night with a load of turnips and we're starting back for Lincolnshire in an hour. We'll take you — they'll never find you down there!

LEVET: Come out, Frank, and talk to the girl. Don't you want to go to Lincolnshire?

ABIGAIL: You've put a spell on him, you devil, you and this old witch here!

ANNA WILLIAMS: Stop this disturbance, girl! The Doctor —

JOHNSON'S VOICE: Frank!

ANNA WILLIAMS: There! You have disturbed the Doctor!

ABIGAIL: [*pounding on the cupboard door*] Frank! Frank! Open the cupboard or I'll break it down!

LEVET: This is getting better all the time.

FRANK: Go away, Abigail. Go back to the country without me. I'm not a turnip.

ABIGAIL: They've bewitched you! I know they have! Help! Help! Sorceress! Kidnappers! Slave-traders!

JOHNSON: Frank!

ANNA WILLIAMS: Stop it, girl, in heaven's name stop it!

FRANK: Go away, Abigail!

[LEVET *laughs again.*]

ABIGAIL: Thieves! Kidnappers! Let Frank go! He's coming with me!

[ABIGAIL's *voice fades during the last speech.*]

LEVET: Ay. She was a right little hell-cat. And the Lord knows how many more of 'em he led up the garden path, that we never knew about.

ANNA WILLIAMS: He was incorrigible. Before he met Betsy, who I grant was the salvation of him...

BETSY'S VOICE: [*persuasive, not harsh*] Frank, you must settle down.

ANNA WILLIAMS: ...he seemed powerless to resist... temptations of that nature.

FRANK: Resist them? I ran towards them. The wonderful times I had with girls — they were the only thing that made my life bearable.

LEVET: Your life was all right. If you look at it straight, it was quite an easy life.

FRANK: I know it was. Lying here, looking back on it, I can see I had a pretty good life. But while I was having it... I just didn't like it.

ANNA WILLIAMS: Why weren't you contented, Frank? I could never understand.

LEVET: Ingratitude. Laziness. It's easy enough to understand.

FRANK: I know that's what you always thought. But somehow, it wasn't as simple as that... I think it was something to do with... the way it all started.

LEVET: When Bathurst handed you over, you mean?

FRANK: Yes, and... before that...

> [*The sound of a plantation bell; black voices chant a work-song; gulls perhaps.* COLONEL BATHURST *is being shown over the plantation where* FRANK *works, by the owner.*]

OWNER: Keep them at it, now: I want those two ships loaded by the early tide tomorrow, so all this field'll have to be picked. Keep them at it. Step this way, Colonel Bathurst. It'll be a pleasure to show you over the plantation. As you see, cotton on this side, tobacco and maize over there.

> [*Throughout this conversation there are background noises of work: the rustle of sheaves, occasional crack of a whip, general rhythmic stirring.*]

BATHURST: I'm glad you invited me. I've spent my life in the army, doing what I could for the success of British military expeditions and the spread of our power and influence, and I'm interested to see just what we're doing with that power and influence.

OWNER: Oh, great things, sir, great things. The slaves are good workers, the climate is just about perfect, and the crops are worth a good deal of money.

BATHURST: Yes... that isn't quite what I had in mind.

OWNER: Keep them at it, overseer. That's my right-hand man supervising them now. He's been my chief overseer for years. Excellent man.

BATHURST: That's a fearsome-looking whip he's carrying. Does he use it much?

OWNER: Oh, slaves get very lazy if you don't tickle them with the whip now and then. And insolent too. They can be very provoking sometimes.

BATHURST: And then they get flogged.

OWNER: They don't mind it, you know. They're built like animals. You wouldn't hesitate to whip a horse, well, it's only the same thing.

BATHURST: I see there are some quite young children working here.

OWNER: Yes, they can start on the simpler parts of the job at about four or five. Before that, they scare birds. We can't have them eating their heads off, you know.

BATHURST: This little fellow here... What's his name?

OWNER: I expect my overseer knows, but I don't. What's your name, boy?

[FRANK *(as child) utters a frightened whimper.*]

OWNER: Your name, boy. The gentleman wants to know your name.

FRANK: [*as child*] Frank, massa.

BATHURST: Your name is Frank. Frank what?

OWNER: Slaves don't have surnames, sir.

BATHURST: So you're just little Frank. How old are you, Frank?

FRANK: [*as child*] I don't know, massa.

BATHURST: Do his parents know how old he is?

OWNER: His mother may be able to remember. I doubt if he knows his father. We don't keep slaves in couples, we keep them in groups of twenty or thirty.

BATHURST: Come here, Frank. Don't be afraid. May I ask you, sir, what you paid for him?

OWNER: I didn't pay anything for him, sir. His mother brought him forth naturally. Of course both she and he, and the father, whichever of them it is, have cost me a pretty penny in food. And I had to rebuild their living quarters last year, after a typhoon knocked everything down; they cost me a fortune, sir, I can assure you.

BATHURST: Let me put it another way. What would this child fetch on the market?

OWNER: About ten pounds, I suppose.

BATHURST: Well, sir, I have ten pounds in my purse here. I have a fancy to become the owner of this boy, if you'll sell him.

OWNER: I thought the Army was already provided with servants.

BATHURST: My active career is nearly over, sir. In a few months I return to England, to retire on half-pay. A little black servant would be useful to me and would cheer my lonely hearth.

OWNER: Well, sir, I can hardly resist that. We have plenty of young boys at present... you wouldn't rather have a girl, would you? A nice plump one about sixteen years old? They can be very comforting. No? Well, it would be more expensive for you, I suppose.

BATHURST: May I give you the ten pounds now?

OWNER: Oh, there's no need to pay me on the spot. Send the money up to the house tonight when you send someone to collect the boy.

BATHURST: I can't... take him now, then?

OWNER: He must finish his day's work, sir. There are two ships in the harbour waiting to be filled. These slaves all ate a meal at mid-day, and the energy that meal gave them, the strength it put into their muscles, belongs by right to me. I'm sure, sir, you see the justice of that.

BATHURST: Yes, sir, I see it.

[*Black voices in work-song.*]

[*Back to voices of adult* FRANK *and* LEVET.]

LEVET: Yes, Bathurst rescued you, he paid ten pounds for you
so that you could live your life as a free man in England
instead of a slave in Jamaica, and I'll be quite frank with
you, there were times when I couldn't see as you were
worth ten pounds of anybody's money. But he did it.

FRANK: Free! So that I could live free! I tell you, it never felt like
freedom.

[FRANK's *mind echoes to a tumult of voices.*]

BETSY: Frank, you must settle down.

LEVET: Always had the best of everything.

ANNA WILLIAMS: The priceless gift of education.

LEVET: Parcels of stinking fish everywhere.

BETSY: Ask the Doctor about getting married. He won't refuse.

ANNA WILLIAMS: And the even more priceless gift of the
Doctor's instruction.

LEVET: Send him to school to learn to be idle.

BETSY: The Doctor doesn't like these scrapes you get into.

ANNA WILLIAMS: Betsy, who I grant was the salvation of him.

LEVET: Too proud to get his hands dirty now he's been to
school.

BETSY: Frank, you must settle down.

ANNA WILLIAMS: The Doctor's priceless gift.

LEVET: Parcels of stinking fish.

BETSY: The Doctor knows what's best.

ANNA WILLIAMS: Priceless gift of knowledge.

LEVET: Even the cat has to wait.

FRANK: [*in a sudden shout*] STOP IT, ALL OF YOU!
[*Abrupt silence.*]

3. *The London house of* COLONEL BATHURST. *The door-bell rings.*

BATHURST: You'd better answer the door-bell, Frank. It may be
Dr Richard — I'm expecting him.

FRANK: [*as child*] Yes, Colonel, sir.
[*Feet on stairs. Door opening. Voice of* RICHARD

BATHURST, *distant — we are hearing him from up-stairs and he is at the street door.*]

RICHARD: Good afternoon, Frank.

FRANK: Good afternoon, Dr Richard.

RICHARD: Is my father in?

FRANK: Yes, sir.

BATHURST: Is that you, Richard?

RICHARD: Yes, father.

BATHURST: Come and sit down, my boy. It's always a pleasure to see you. I know a young doctor, with a London practice to build up, can't always spare time to visit an aged parent.

RICHARD: Oh, come, father, not so aged.

BATHURST: Worn out, my boy, aged or not, worn out.

RICHARD: Oh, I wouldn't say that.

BATHURST: You can't be much of a doctor if you can't see I'm worn out.

RICHARD: No, perhaps I'm not much of a doctor.

BATHURST: What d'you mean by that?

RICHARD: [*sighs*] Oh, well... Had you something special to talk about, father, that you sent for me?

BATHURST: Yes, my boy. I wanted to talk about... putting things in order.

RICHARD: Things in order? What things?

BATHURST: [*with a flash of irritation*] Everything, of course, I'm dying, dammit.

RICHARD: Well, if you say so...

BATHURST: You're a strange kind of doctor, Richard.

RICHARD: Perhaps I am. Or rather perhaps I was.

BATHURST: What d'you mean, was?

RICHARD: I'm giving up, father. I've failed. My London practice is... just no good. I've been trying for a year and I'm still not paying my expenses.

BATHURST: But why, why?

RICHARD: Oh, I just haven't got the right bedside manner, I suppose. I know medicine pretty well, but I haven't got the art of selling myself to the people with the money. Knowing when to frighten them and when to soothe them, making three visits where one would do and charging them half-a-guinea a time, all that... I'm giving up. The practice closes down next week.

BATHURST: And what will you do?

RICHARD: I shall go into the Navy.

BATHURST: The Navy? Why not the Army?

RICHARD: No special reason. Wanted to be different from you, I suppose.

BATHURST: Oh, well, it should be just as easy to keep Frank with you.

RICHARD: Keep Frank with me?

BATHURST: Yes. A naval surgeon'll be allowed to take his own personal attendant on board, if he speaks to the right people.

RICHARD: But Frank isn't my personal attendant. He's your servant.

BATHURST: I shan't need a servant where I'm going, Richard, and Frank's got to be looked after somehow.

RICHARD: Let me get this straight. You want me to take Frank as my servant, even if it means taking him on board a man-of-war?

BATHURST: I want you to be ready to take Frank when I go, which I expect will be some time this winter.

RICHARD: Unless you have plans to blow your brains out on a certain date, father, you can't predict when you'll go. And when the time comes, I might be on one of His Majesty's ships, three months' voyage away on the other side of the world.

BATHURST: Well, Frank could wait here till you got back. He could write you a letter with the news. I've had him educated, he's literate.

RICHARD: Look, father, you don't own Frank.

BATHURST: In a sense, of course, you're quite wrong. I do own him. I paid £10 for him in Jamaica.

RICHARD: But you know what I mean. Neither you nor I believe slavery is right. We don't believe one human being can own another.

BATHURST: That's true, my boy.

RICHARD: Have you consulted Frank? Have you asked him whether he wants to sail with the Navy?

BATHURST: He'll be all right if he's with you.

RICHARD: He'll be on a ship. You know what Sam Johnson says about ships? [*He imitates* JOHNSON'S *voice*.] 'No man, Sir, will go to sea who has contrivance enough to get himself into gaol. For being at sea is being in gaol, with a chance of being drowned.'

BATHURST: And who might this oracle be, this Sam Johnson?

RICHARD: Your memory really is going, isn't it? You had dinner at the Mitre not two months ago, and Sam Johnson was there.

BATHURST: Oh, yes, the big fellow with a twitch.

RICHARD: Is that all you remember about Sam Johnson?

BATHURST: Why, what should I remember?

RICHARD: Nothing, except that — setting aside the reverence I have for you as my own father — Sam Johnson is the best and wisest man I have ever known.

BATHURST: H'm, that's interesting. But to get back to Frank —

RICHARD: I haven't got away from Frank, father. While we've been talking I've been thinking, and I've had a wonderful idea.

BATHURST: As wonderful as your idea of closing down your practice and joining the Navy?

RICHARD: That's not an idea, it's stark necessity. But this is an idea, and an excellent one. We'll try to get Sam Johnson to take Frank into his household.

BATHURST: Oh, I hardly think that would do.

RICHARD: What could you possibly have against it?

BATHURST: Surely we can do better for Frank than that? If you can't take him —

RICHARD: Do better, yes, we can do better. We can get him into some rich, fashionable household where they'll make a pet of him as a sweet woolly-haired piccaninny, and then get tired of him and throw him on to the street when he gets big and ungainly to live by thievery and end up on the gallows.

BATHURST: Still, there's no need to go to the other extreme.

RICHARD: What other extreme?

BATHURST: From what I remember about Mr Johnson, his person is so slovenly that his house must be squalid to match it. Surely we can find Frank a better —

RICHARD: If Johnson's clothes need brushing and his house needs cleaning, all the more reason for him to have a servant. Besides, this is the right time to ask him. His wife's died, and he's very lonely.

BATHURST: So you propose to put Frank into a bereaved, grief-stricken house, dirty and neglected, with a —

RICHARD: [*interrupting*] Hush — be quiet a moment, please.

BATHURST: I won't be quiet, Richard. I may not be here much longer to speak my mind. You want to put Frank into a house like that, with a careless, grubby old philosopher who twitches and drops his food on the floor.

> [*Quick footsteps, the noise of a door being wrenched open, a sudden scuffling sound. And* FRANK's *startled cry.*]

RICHARD: All right, Frank, keep still and I'll let go of your ear... there.

FRANK: Dr Richard — don't be angry —

RICHARD: I have sharp ears, Frank. I heard the stairs creak even under your small weight.

BATHURST: Bless my soul, was the boy eavesdropping? Come, Frank, I expected better of you.

FRANK: [*weeping*] But you and Dr Richard was talking of me, Colonel, sir. I heard my name, sir.

BATHURST: [*severely*] Well, sir, and what if you did hear your name? Who is going to discuss your welfare and make plans for you if I am not — I and Dr Richard?

FRANK: That's just it, sir. [*He weeps.*]

BATHURST: What do you mean, boy, that's just it?

FRANK: I heard you making plans, sir, and I was —

BATHURST: Well, you were what?

FRANK: [*sobbing*] Frightened, Colonel, sir. I was frightened!

RICHARD: There's nothing to be frightened of, Frank. We're going to put you with a very kind gentleman, who'll look after you.

FRANK: I don't want to go to him!

RICHARD: Don't be silly, Frank, you don't even know him.

FRANK: I heard you talking about him, Dr Richard, and I'm frightened. I don't want to go to him and his dark house!

RICHARD: His house isn't darker than anyone else's, Frank. It may be a bit dusty, but you can look after that.

FRANK: I don't want to go! I want to stay with the Colonel! He's the kindest gentleman in the world! He took me away from the plantation where they used to whip me! Colonel, I want to stay with you... [*His voice is drowned in weeping.*]

4. Street sounds. FRANK *and* RICHARD BATHURST *are approaching* DR JOHNSON's *house in Gough Square. They knock at the door and wait.*

RICHARD: [*kindly*] Now, Frank, remember, you have nothing to be afraid of in Dr Johnson's house. Quite the contrary. You have everything to gain here.
[*The door is opened.*]

LEVET: Oh, it's you.

RICHARD: [*pleasantly*] Good afternoon, Levet. Would you be so kind as to tell Dr Johnson that we have come to see him as arranged?

LEVET: I'm not a servant, let's get that straight.

RICHARD: [*still pleasant*] Very well, I will go up and tell him myself. I know my way in this house.

LEVET: Ay. There's too many as does that. The Doctor never gets a bit of peace.
[*We hear* RICHARD's *footsteps as he goes down to the kitchen.*]

RICHARD: Good afternoon, Miss Williams. You're looking well today. And your usual queenly self. [*He kisses her hand.*]

ANNA WILLIAMS: Good day, Dr Bathurst. It's always a pleasure to receive you.

LEVET: [*who has been scrutinizing* FRANK *in no flattering way*] Who's your friend, Mr Bathurst?

RICHARD: [*pleasantly*] Dr Bathurst, if you please, Mr Levet.

LEVET: No man as doesn't give me my right title gets his. I'm known from Seven Dials to Islington as Dr Levet.

RICHARD: [*tolerantly*] Oh, excuse me. Dr Levet. What was it you wanted to ask me?

LEVET: I said, who's your friend. We haven't been introduced.

RICHARD: This little chap is Frank Barber, at present in the employment of my father, Colonel Bathurst. Frank, this is Dr Levet, of whom you have heard me speak.

LEVET: [*nodding to himself*] Colonel Bathurst. Ah, that explains it.

RICHARD: Explains what?

LEVET: How it came about.

RICHARD: How what came about?

LEVET: We're both men of the world. We're broad-minded — we have to be, in our job.

RICHARD: Could I possibly prevail on you to tell me what you're talking about?

LEVET: Your dad... all those years a serving soldier.

RICHARD: [*beginning to see his drift, dangerously polite*] What of them?

LEVET: In those tropical countries. Shimmering heat. Passions rising to the surface unbidden. Not like here where you have to haul them up with a bucket.

RICHARD: Go on.

LEVET: Like I say, we're tolerant in our profession. Broad-minded. We know the effect of the climate on passions.

RICHARD: Dr Levet, I hope for your sake that you are not making some low insinuation about my respected father.

ANNA WILLIAMS: Ignore him, Dr Bathurst, ignore the low-bred fellow, it's the only way.

LEVET: Don't tell me. All those years in the tropics. Can't take your wife with you. British Army personnel aren't allowed to take wives and children on tropical service. So what happens? All those darky women everywhere, and God made 'em the right shape and size: a man's got to live. So of course they come back with a little souvenir now and again. Let's have a look at you, Sambo.

RICHARD: His name is not Sambo, it is Frank, and he is not the illegitimate son of my father by a native concubine. I warn you, Levet, to stop there. Only the fact that you are so many years my senior has prevented me from knocking you down already.

LEVET: Don't worry about my age. Come on any time you like. Only watch yourself. I learnt my fighting in the back streets of Paris. [*He squares up.*]

ANNA WILLIAMS: Heaven preserve us, what an example to set this poor heathen child!

LEVET: Mr Bathurst, if you've come to see the Doctor, go up and see him. He's in, working away at his Dictionary. Just don't expect me to show you up and announce you because I'm not a servant.

RICHARD: [*thoughtfully*] No. If it comes to that I don't suppose the Doctor has got a servant?

LEVET: There's a woman as comes in to scrub. And another to wash the clothes, not that the Doctor bothers her much. He usually wears 'em till you have to cut 'em off.

RICHARD: Well, if all goes well, he'll have a servant soon — a bright, pleasant, willing little fellow who'll make his life more comfortable.

LEVET: A servant?

RICHARD: Frank.

LEVET: [*after a pause*] Has he said he wants a servant?

RICHARD: No. But then Dr Johnson never says he wants anything. He's sublimely indifferent to this own comforts and conveniences.

LEVET: And to everyone else's. The house is a bear-garden already, without turning it into a darkies' orphanage as well.

ANNA WILLIAMS: Mr Levet, you are insufferable!

LEVET: So they tell me, ma'am.

RICHARD: Levet, I'm sorry to find you in this obstructive and cynical mood. You should let some of the Doctor's generosity rub off on you.

LEVET: The only thing he's got that's likely to rub off on me is his dandruff.

RICHARD: I shall waste no further time on you. I'm going up to
see Dr Johnson now, and [*turning to* MISS WILLIAMS] I shall
leave Frank with you, Miss Williams. I know you will be
kind to him. Stay here till I come down, Frank, and be a
good boy.

[RICHARD *is heard going upstairs. Short silence.*]

ANNA WILLIAMS: Come here, child. Nearer. Nearer. I need to
touch you, I cannot see, but I can tell what you are like if
I touch you, quite gently... so. Woolly hair, African
features... so. What did Dr Bathurst say your name was,
child?

FRANK: Frank, madam.

ANNA WILLIAMS: Who taught you that when you speak to ladies
you must address them as madam?

FRANK: Colonel Bathurst, madam.

ANNA WILLIAMS: That is right and you have been well brought
up. But you must call me Miss Williams.

[FRANK *is silent.*]

ANNA WILLIAMS: What must you call me?

FRANK: Miss Williams, madam.

ANNA WILLIAMS: Miss Anna Williams. You will need to know my
name, Frank. I have almost as many visitors as the
Doctor, and you will be answering the door.

FRANK: Yes, mad— Miss Williams.

ANNA WILLIAMS: I am the most important person in this household, Frank, no matter who tells you anything else.

LEVET: [*to ceiling*] Nobody tells me anything.

ANNA WILLIAMS: Apart of course from Dr Johnson himself.
Dr Johnson is a great man, Frank. He does very impor-
tant work. At the present time he is writing a dictionary.
Do you know what a dictionary is, Frank?

FRANK: No, Miss Williams.

ANNA WILLIAMS: It is a big book that gathers together all the
words in the language and explains what they mean. So
you see how important that is. To write a dictionary you
have to know everything. [*She waits for his reaction, but
none comes.*] Can you read, Frank?

FRANK: Yes, Miss Williams.

ANNA WILLIAMS: Then you will be able to consult Dr Johnson's dictionary when it is finished. If I use a word you don't understand, the dictionary will tell you what it means. So if I say to you that you are privileged to be the servant of a man as great as the Doctor, if you don't understand the word 'privileged', you can look it up and then you will know. Do you know what the word 'privileged' means, Frank?

FRANK: No, Miss Williams.

LEVET: It means having letters after your name.

ANNA WILLIAMS: It means exceptionally fortunate, Frank. A privileged person enjoys blessings that other people do not enjoy. 'Privileged' means 'singled out for specially good treatment or special honours'. If the Doctor agrees to have you come and live here and be his servant, Frank, you will be privileged. Specially honoured.

FRANK: [*in a sudden outburst*] I don't want to be prilliveged. [*sic*]

ANNA WILLIAMS: You don't want to be?

FRANK: I want to stay with Colonel Bathurst. He's the gentleman that took me away from that place where they whipped me and made me work in the fields. He's the gentleman that looks after me and I feel happy with him. That's prillivege [*sic*] enough for me, madam.

ANNA WILLIAMS: Miss Williams.

FRANK: Miss Williams. I don't want to come here and never see the Colonel again.

ANNA WILLIAMS: Frank, you must not say such things. You are a little boy, and what is more a little black boy, born without any understanding of the world.

LEVET: I suppose you were born reading a dictionary.

ANNA WILLIAMS: Other people know what is best for you, Frank, and you don't know what is best for yourself. If Dr Johnson is willing to take you, you will be very privileged.

LEVET: That's one word he's never going to look up. He'll hate it too much.

ANNA WILLIAMS: Dr Johnson is very wise, Frank, and he is a great man. But even great men are human beings like ourselves. Dr Johnson has many sorrows and troubles.

They prey on his mind, Frank, and he cannot sleep at night. He is afraid to go to bed, very often, and he stays out late with his friends. And when he does come back he needs someone to talk to him and to serve him tea.

LEVET: Tea and talk, tea and talk! He'd be better off in bed with a woman!

ANNA WILLIAMS: You must try not to be influenced by Mr Levet, Frank. He has his good qualities, but he is a rough man — the product of a rough upbringing. Dr Johnson has been a very sad man since his wife died.

LEVET: Go on, start building her up now. The poor little devil can't contradict you.

ANNA WILLIAMS: Thank you, Mr Levet, there is no reason why he should contradict me, since I am telling him the truth. Dr Johnson, Frank, is a gentle and sensitive man. Many people do not think so. They are misled by his appearance. He is very big and — some people have found, on first sight — rather frightening. His voice is a trifle loud.

LEVET: Why not tell him he eats little black boys and have done with it?

ANNA WILLIAMS: Under his formidable exterior, Frank, Dr Johnson is the kindest man in the world. But I hear footsteps on the stairs. Dr Bathurst is coming down. I hope for your sake, Frank, that he is bringing good news for you — that you will be allowed to stay here.

FRANK: I want to go back to the Colonel.

ANNA WILLIAMS: Hush, Frank.

LEVET: Listen, lad, if you go back to the Colonel you'll be out of a job in three months. I saw the Colonel in the street the other day and he's a dead pigeon. I know cardiac degeneration when I see it, even if I'm not qualified. [*His last words are directed savagely at* MISS WILLIAMS.]

[RICHARD *enters.*]

RICHARD: Frank, you're a lucky boy. I told Dr Johnson all about you, and he listened very carefully, especially to the part about your having been born in slavery. 'I hate a slave-trader,' says he, 'as I hate a fiend of hell. Show me the boy,' says he, 'bring him upstairs and show him to me, and if I take to him the least bit, he shall enter my household and live here.'

FRANK: Will he take to me, Mr Richard?

RICHARD: Of course he will, Frank. Everybody takes to you. You're a nice little chap. Just give the Doctor a big smile, and you'll win his heart.

ANNA WILLIAMS: And there's no prize more worth winning in the whole world.

RICHARD: Well, come along, Frank. Don't keep the Doctor waiting.

FRANK: Do I have to come, Mr Richard?

RICHARD: [*bending down to him, speaking gently*] Yes, Frank, you have to come. It's the best thing for you. I can't look after you because I'm going away on a big ship, and I can't take you with me.

FRANK: I'd like to go on a big ship. I could work and be useful. Why can't you take me?

RICHARD: No, I can't, Frank, and you can't stay with my father the Colonel, because he's going away soon.

FRANK: Going away? Where to? I could go with him, Mr Richard, I could help him.

RICHARD: You can't help him where he's going now. We must be glad about it, Frank. My father is going to his Father, who is in Heaven.

FRANK: And I have to stay here? And never see you or the Colonel again?

RICHARD: You'll see me again sometimes, Frank. I'll come and visit you. But come along now, to meet the Doctor.

[RICHARD *moves off;* FRANK *reluctantly follows in his wake. As they near the door,* MISS WILLIAMS *calls out after them.*]

ANNA WILLIAMS: Mind your manners, Frank, and don't forget to give the Doctor a big smile.

[*Footsteps. The door closes. A burst of* LEVET's *rusty laughter.*]

ANNA WILLIAMS: Is there any point, Mr Levet, in asking what it is that you find amusing?

LEVET: I don't want to rub it in, but a blind person misses a lot of amusing things.

ANNA WILLIAMS: No doubt.

LEVET: Mind you, I don't know whether you'd have been amused by what I've just seen. But I was, heh, heh. You see — when you told the little darky to mind his manners, he turned round and pulled a face at you. He stuck his thumbs in his ears and waggled his fingers about and pulled a terrible face.

ANNA WILLIAMS: Poor child. His education into civilized ways has a long way to go yet.

LEVET: Neither you or I'll live to see him civilized.

5. FRANK *has now an adult voice. He is a well-grown youth, lounging about in the street outside* DR JOHNSON'*s house. This is conveyed by street noises. Sound of door opening.* LEVET *has come out.*

LEVET: What d'you think you're doing?

FRANK: Leaning against these railings.

LEVET: Don't strain yourself, will you?

FRANK: I've got a right to some time off.

LEVET: Time off's one thing. Propping up the street railings in the middle of the morning's another.

FRANK: I like it out in the street, in the summer time. There's not so many flies out here as there is in the house.

LEVET: There's flies in the house because you leave remains of food about. You haven't washed the dishes from last night yet. And another thing. That damn' great bundle of fish on the kitchen table. It's going off.

FRANK: It don't matter if that goes off. It's just oysters for the cat. The Doctor brings 'em in.

LEVET: Why doesn't the cat eat 'em, then, and get rid of the smell?

FRANK: He'll eat 'em when I put 'em in his dish. And that'll be in my good time.

LEVET: Seven years you've been supposed to work here, and

the place is more of a pigsty with every day that goes by. If I was the Doctor I'd sack you.

FRANK: But you're not the Doctor, are you?

[*Footsteps.* LEVET *goes.* FRANK *soliloquizes at his receding back view.*]

FRANK: Trot along, old Levet, trot along. I got a good reason for being out in the street, just at this time. [*His voice becomes urgent.*] And here she comes! It's her all right!

[*Light feminine footsteps.*]

FRANK: Can I help you, Missy? Can I carry the bundle for you?

BETSY: [*coolly*] I can manage, thank you.

FRANK: Where are you taking it?

BETSY: That's my business, isn't it?

FRANK: Ah, don't be like that.

BETSY: What's it got to do with you what I'm like? Look, stand out of the way and let me get on. My mother's waiting for this lot. She's got to have it washed and delivered back by five o'clock.

FRANK: That's the business you're in, is it? Washing clothes?

BETSY: It's the business my mother's in. It's all right when you get to her age.

FRANK: What's all right?

BETSY: Getting your hands all crinkly and bending over the tub with the steam making your face red and raking all the curl out of your hair. I'm not going to do that — I've still got a use for my looks.

FRANK: [*admiringly*] You bet you have.

BETSY: Not what you mean, either. I'm going to be a lady's maid. They have to be neat and pretty.

FRANK: Going to be? Why aren't you one already?

BETSY: I'm waiting for the right vacancy. And meanwhile I help my mother with the deliveries.

FRANK: I know why you haven't got a job yet. You're too pretty for a lady's maid. These ladies like to employ girls who look nice but not too nice, else they take all the attention away from the lady.

BETSY: Of course, you know all about it, don't you? Stand out of the way, will you?

FRANK: Yes, I do know about it. That's the game I'm in myself. Domestic service.

BETSY: I know. You're Dr Johnson's boy. I've seen you with him.

FRANK: Oh, well. I wish I was anybody else's boy, sometimes.

BETSY: Why, does he treat you bad?

FRANK: Don't make me laugh. I wouldn't let anyone treat me bad. No, I stay with poor old Johnson because he needs me. But I don't like it. It makes me embarrassed with his funny ways. I could sink through the floor sometimes, he makes such a spectacle of himself. I hate going anywhere with him.

BETSY: He does look a bit peculiar. And those jerky movements he keeps making.

FRANK: It's awful. Whenever he goes out a crowd gets round him. They think he's a wild man advertising a circus. And when they see a black chap with him they know he's advertising a circus.

BETSY: I shouldn't let it get you down too much. There's plenty of black fellows in service.

FRANK: Yes, but not with freaks like him.

BETSY: Well, I can't stand here all day. This bundle's pulling my arms out.

FRANK: Well, let me carry it for you.

BETSY: No.

FRANK: What's the matter? I ain't good enough for you, I suppose?

BETSY: I didn't say that.

FRANK: No, but it's what you meant.

BETSY: My mother sent me out to fetch this washing, not to hang about in the street with fellows.

FRANK: Are you going home now?

BETSY: What's it to you?

FRANK: 'Cause I'm going to follow you and see where you live.

BETSY: Don't you dare!

FRANK: I will too.

[FRANK *is remembering all this as he lies in his bed in Stafford Infirmary.*]

FRANK: Ah, Betsy was lovely. I had to work hard to get her. I loved her before she loved me. But then that funny old nature of mine, it kind of took over. Once I knew she loved me, once her mind was made up that it was Frank Barber she wanted, I started making her work hard.

[*Back to narrative time.*]

BETSY: Frank, you must settle down.

FRANK: I know, I know.

BETSY: Your wild ways are getting you talked about.

FRANK: Getting me talked about! I don't hear that. Nobody talks about me. There ain't such a person as Frank Barber. I'm just Dr Johnson's boy.

BETSY: It's not true, Frank, but even if it was true, you can change it. If you think people only see you as Dr Johnson's boy, you can be somebody else as well.

FRANK: Who else can I be?

BETSY: You can be Betsy Barber's husband, that's who. You can have a wife and a family to look up to you.

FRANK: [*thoughtfully*] A wife and a family. Is it nice having a family, Betsy?

BETSY: They can be annoying sometimes, but mostly it's very nice. And anyway it's the only way to live.

FRANK: You see... I didn't have a family. Not the way you mean. It was... different.

[*Plantation sounds: children's voices in some kind of singing game.*]

FRANK: It was different. But... it stayed with me. I carried it inside me. I carried a world inside me that I couldn't quite remember. But I know it gave me... different feelings.

BETSY: Frank, you must settle now. I love you and I'll give you children who'll love you.

FRANK: I've always felt different. I used to lie awake at night and stare up at the ceiling and wonder where I could find my own people, the ones I belonged with, the ones who had the same world inside them as I had.

> [*Music now indicates that* FRANK *has mentally moved from the plantation to being on board ship. Men's voices in shanty or similar nautical work-song; and gulls, if the effect does not turn out to be too obvious. Shanty ends. Silence.*]

6. *Hurrying feet: they are* BETSY's. *She is making for* JOHNSON's *house in search of* FRANK. *Street door opening, footsteps on stairs.*

ANNA WILLIAMS: Who is that in such haste?

LEVET: You don't usually let yourself in, lass. You normally have the manners to knock.

BETSY: I just couldn't wait, Dr Levet. I'm in such a state about Frank. Is he back yet?

LEVET: Not to say back, no.

BETSY: But what can have happened to him? He's been away four days now!

LEVET: Well, as it happens, lass, we've had news today and we're in a position to tell you what's happened to him.

BETSY: What's happened then? What?

LEVET: [*slowly and impressively*] He's gone mad.

BETSY: What?

LEVET: He's gone raving mad.

BETSY: Oh, whatever d'you... Is he in Bedlam?

LEVET: Worse than that.

BETSY: Worse?

LEVET: Much worse than Bedlam where he is.

ANNA WILLIAMS: Levet, stop tormenting the girl and tell her the news.

LEVET: I'm telling her as fast as I can, if you'd both stop interrupting. Here it is then. He's joined the Navy.

BETSY: Joined... the Navy?

LEVET: Joined the Navy and gone to sea.

BETSY: Oh, Frank! [*She weeps.*]

> [*Shanty. Sea and ship sounds. Silence.*]

7. BETSY *is hurrying towards the street door at Gough Square. She knocks. Slow, reluctant footsteps heard within: they are* LEVET's. *She knocks again.*

LEVET: All right, all right. [*He opens the door.*] Well, what do you want?

BETSY: What do I want, Dr Levet? What do I ever want?

LEVET: I was hoping it was something different for once.

BETSY: No, it isn't something different.

LEVET: And my answer isn't any different either. It's no. I haven't got any news of Frank. None of us have heard anything.

BETSY: [*despondent*] Oh.

LEVET: How much longer are you going to go on pestering about him. He's gone, hasn't he?

BETSY: But surely the Doctor —

LEVET: The Doctor what?

BETSY: The Doctor knows a lot of important people. He knows Lords and judges and — all those sort. He could get Frank out.

LEVET: P'raps he doesn't want to get Frank out.

BETSY: Miss Williams says the Doctor misses Frank.

LEVET: Miss Williams, Miss Williams.

BETSY: Can I come in, please? I want to go down and see Miss Williams.

LEVET: You won't get anything out of her.

BETSY: It's not to get anything out of her. You know I come to see her nearly every day, to know if she wants anything from the shops.

LEVET: All right, come in. I'm going upstairs where I don't have to listen to your chatter.

[BETSY *goes downstairs.*]

ANNA WILLIAMS: Is that Betsy?

BETSY: Yes, Miss Williams.

ANNA WILLIAMS: I haven't any errands today, Betsy. You're a kind girl.

BETSY: I'm a sad girl, too, Miss Williams, and a lonely girl.

ANNA WILLIAMS: I know you're sad, Betsy, but... lonely?

BETSY: Why d'you ask that?

ANNA WILLIAMS: Things come to me as I sit here in my darkness. I never go anywhere, but because I keep still the world comes to me.

BETSY: And?

ANNA WILLIAMS: [*gently*] Betsy, you've been seen walking out with a lot of young men in this neighbourhood.

BETSY: Yes, a lot.

ANNA WILLIAMS: A girl can lose her good name.

BETSY: Look, Miss Williams, I don't know about good names but I know what it is to wake up crying in the night. Frank's been gone for nearly two years now and I still wake crying.

ANNA WILLIAMS: I know. I believe you.

BETSY: So of course I go round with a lot of fellows. I'm trying to find one that suits me. So I can forget about Frank. The way he's forgotten about me. He must have done. He never writes. [*Her tone changes: soft, wistful.*] Miss Williams, d'you think he has forgotten about me?

ANNA WILLIAMS: How can anyone tell, Betsy? He may be trying to, just as you're trying to forget about him, and neither of you succeeding.

BETSY: [*passionately*] But when shall I ever see him again, to find out? When, when, when?

ANNA WILLIAMS: You must leave it in the hands of God, my girl.

BETSY: If I could find a fellow I really liked, I'd snap my fingers at Frank. But I can't do it. Frank always comes back into my mind. Miss Williams, why does Frank always come back into my mind?

ANNA WILLIAMS: Your love will be rewarded, Betsy. Some-where, somehow. I feel certain of that.

BETSY: I hope you don't mean a crown in heaven. I want it on earth. I want Frank. I want Frank. I want Frank.

8. On board ship in harbour. Voices calling...

1ST VOICE: Barber to report to Captain's cabin.

2ND VOICE: Barber to report to Captain's cabin.

[*Knock on door.*]

CAPTAIN: Come in.

FRANK: [*entering*] You sent for me, Captain, sir.

CAPTAIN: Yes, Barber. [*Pause.*] I was talking about you the other day. To the Chaplain.

FRANK: The Chaplain, sir? I hope I haven't been doing wrong.

CAPTAIN: It depends on what you think wrong, Barber. [*Pause.*] The Chaplain tells me you're a well-taught young fellow. Well-taught from his point of view, that is: in the scriptures. He says you know your Bible well, and your Prayer Book.

FRANK: Yes, sir. [*Pause.*] Will that be all, sir?

CAPTAIN: No, Barber. You can stand there while I collect my thoughts. I'm trying to piece together what kind of background you have and why you decided to join the Navy.

FRANK: I wanted to be a sailor, sir.

CAPTAIN: You wanted to be a sailor. [*Pause.*] We know you as an educated lad, Barber, you've had much more book learning than most of the men who come in on lower deck. That's why you do a clerking job, sitting in comparative comfort with the chief quartermaster and the purser, instead of shinning up the masts and running along the yard-arms all day and half the night like the rest of the crew.

FRANK: Ay, ay, sir.

CAPTAIN: Most of the men who join this ship, Barber, or any ship, do it because they're grabbed by the press-gang and put in irons till we're well out to sea, or because they're on the run from the law. A few join to get a square meal, but most men would rather be very, very hungry than put themselves aboard a ship of the line. I make a practice of not getting to know the men under my command at all closely. I don't know their individual names, and as far as possible I try not to notice their individual faces, or I might have them coming a little too close to me in my dreams. It's a hard life we give them, and sometimes we don't even give them that. I don't need to tell you, Barber, because you've been in the Navy a couple of years now, that on a long voyage we expect to lose about a third of the men. If they don't die in action, they die of various diseases, because the kind of doctoring we can give them, with one surgeon and no orderlies, just isn't enough to keep them alive. Sometimes, Barber, I get all hands on deck just before we weigh anchor, when we've a full muster, and I look at them standing there row upon row, and think to myself that before we see port again the chances are that one in three of those men will be dead and thrown over board. In sure and certain hope of a resurrection to eternal life. You know the Prayer Book well, Barber?

FRANK: Yes, sir.

CAPTAIN: Who taught you?

FRANK: [*hesitantly*] A gentleman I used to work for, sir, before I joined.

CAPTAIN: What gentleman?

FRANK: He was called Dr Johnson, sir.

CAPTAIN: You worked for this Dr Johnson? Doing what, Barber?

FRANK: [*reluctantly*] I was his manservant, sir.

CAPTAIN: You were his manservant. But he had somebody teach you your Bible and Prayer Book.

FRANK: No, sir.

CAPTAIN: What do you mean, no, sir?

FRANK: He taught me himself, sir.

CAPTAIN: You were his servant, his black manservant, but he sat down with you and taught you your Bible and Prayer Book?

FRANK: Yes, sir.

CAPTAIN: Did he teach you to read first?

FRANK: No, sir. I went to school for that.

CAPTAIN: You went to school. Who sent you, and paid the schoolmaster?

FRANK: Dr Johnson, sir.

[*Pause.*]

CAPTAIN: This Dr Johnson, whoever he was, seems to have been very kind to you, Barber.

[FRANK *remains silent.*]

CAPTAIN: I spoke to you, Barber.

FRANK: Ay, ay, sir. He was kind to me, sir.

CAPTAIN: He seems to have taken thought for you, Barber. He seems to have cared what happened to you.

FRANK: Yes, sir.

CAPTAIN: Did you tell him you were going to join the Navy?

FRANK: [*Pause.*] No, sir.

CAPTAIN: You just went. Leaving him to wonder what had happened to you.

FRANK: I sent word, sir.

CAPTAIN: You sent word. That was good of you. Dear Dr Johnson, I have run away from your house and your service, and I have joined the Navy.

FRANK: I wanted to be a sailor, sir. I didn't want to be a servant, sir.

CAPTAIN: You are more a servant here, Barber, than you ever were with him. There are far more people here who can give you orders, and lay a rope's end across your back, than ever could in Dr Johnson's house. And if that's not enough to keep you well disciplined, they have other things they can do. You've seen them done, Barber.

FRANK: Yes, sir.

CAPTAIN: And you'd still rather be on board ship than in Dr Johnson's house.

FRANK: Yes, sir.

CAPTAIN: Well, Barber, that's a pity, because it means I have bad news for you. This Dr Johnson, whoever he may be, seems to be a friend of Mr John Wilkes, and Mr Wilkes is one of the Lords of the Admiralty. He has made a personal request to Mr Wilkes, at the Admiralty, to see

that you are given your discharge. And Mr Wilkes has
obliged.

FRANK: My... discharge, sir?

CAPTAIN: I have the appropriate piece of paper here in my
hand. If you wish to inspect it, that is your right.

FRANK: But... I don't want to be discharged, sir.

CAPTAIN: No-one seems to have troubled much about what you
want, Barber, and I propose to follow that example. You
are no longer a member of His Majesty's Navy.

FRANK: But... Captain.

CAPTAIN: You are a landsman, Barber, a civilian. Collect your
back pay from the purser, and make your arrangements
to leave the ship. If you have nowhere to go you can stay
aboard tonight. But if I see you on the ship after eight
bells tomorrow morning I shall treat you as a trespasser.
        [FRANK *glugs*.]

CAPTAIN: [*more kindly*] You must go back to Dr Johnson,
Barber. I know nothing about him, but to take so much
trouble he must be kind-hearted. Since you have a kind
master, Barber, go back to him. You may never find
another.

FRANK: [*brokenly*] Ay, ay, sir.

CAPTAIN: Here is your discharge, Barber. Go now. You are no
longer under my command. [*As* FRANK *still stands there...*]
Well, go, man, go: has something robbed you of your
power of movement?

FRANK: Yes, sir. That is, no, sir. Ay, ay, Captain, sir.

9. Footsteps heavily descending stairs. LEVET *is going down to the
kitchen, where* MISS WILLIAMS *is sitting. Door slams, petulantly.*

LEVET: Well, the old fool's done it again.

ANNA WILLIAMS: I suppose I must ask you to whom you refer?

LEVET: The old fool upstairs, who else?

ANNA WILLIAMS: Our benefactor, Dr Samuel Johnson, has done
what again?

LEVET: I give up on him. For years I've thought of myself as his medical officer, but I give up now. There are some people you can't protect.

ANNA WILLIAMS: Protect against what, you purposely annoying man?

LEVET: Against their own fatal weaknesses. Our benefactor Dr Samuel Johnson [*savagely mimicking her voice*] has something much more dangerous than a weak heart.

ANNA WILLIAMS: What's that?

LEVET: A kind one.

ANNA WILLIAMS: That is not in dispute.

LEVET: But wait till you hear what it's landed him in now. He's taking Frank back.

ANNA WILLIAMS: From the Navy?

LEVET: From the Navy.

ANNA WILLIAMS: Have they agreed to his discharge?

LEVET: The Doctor's pestered 'em into it. All those letters he's written. And all the time he's been out in the afternoon without saying where he was going — to the Admiralty, I'll be bound. To suck up to Wilkes, a man he hates. And for the sake of that idle, impudent black devil who should have been left where he is.

ANNA WILLIAMS: Betsy will be pleased.

LEVET: Betsy'll be pleased — is that all you can think about? What about the rest of us, having him under our feet again?

ANNA WILLIAMS: You must tell Betsy when you see her.

LEVET: I'll tell nobody. I'm too ashamed of living under the same roof with such foolishness.

[*Nautical music running down into tunelessness.*]

10. FRANK *is back in the kitchen of* DR JOHNSON's *house.*

BETSY: So you're back, Frank.

FRANK: Yes.

BETSY: Are you glad?

FRANK: No.

BETSY: The Navy was all right, was it?

FRANK: All right, yes. [*Pause.*] Why aren't you angry with me?

BETSY: Why should I be ?

FRANK: I go off without a word, I leave you when you're expecting we're going to get married, I stay away two years and when I do come back and you come round to see me, I say I'm not glad.

BETSY: Well, if that's how you feel, what difference would it make if I did get angry?

FRANK: It just — don't seem natural, that's all.

BETSY: You running away to sea, was that natural?

FRANK: In a way it was.

BETSY: Well then. What's the good of being angry with something that's natural?

FRANK: I don't understand you, Betsy.

BETSY: I know you don't.

> [*Pause.*]

FRANK: I s'pose you don't... want to have anything to do with me.

BETSY: Why not?

FRANK: Well, after the way I've acted.

BETSY: You don't act, Frank. Things act on you.

FRANK: Betsy, don't say that. It makes me angry.

BETSY: You see? I'm acting on you.

FRANK: It makes me mad when people treat me like a thing, that's pushed around and moved from place to place, not like a person.

BETSY: So you thought you'd get up and do something. Take a big step. Make everybody think you were a person, with a mind of your own.

FRANK: Yes, yes.

BETSY: Is that true, Frank?

FRANK: Is what true?

BETSY: Is that really how it was?

> [*Pause.*]

FRANK: No.

BETSY: I thought not.

FRANK: Look, Betsy, come and sit close by me.

BETSY: Why?

FRANK: I need to talk to you. I can't get things straight for my-self unless I can talk them out to you.

BETSY: Who did you talk to in the Navy? The ship's cat?

FRANK: I had no call to talk in the Navy. It was action all the time. But listen, I need to tell you how it was.

[*She sits down beside him.*]

BETSY: All right, tell me.

FRANK: [*begins slowly*] It wasn't anything to do with being a person. Making decisions and that stuff. That was just... talk.

BETSY: Well, what was it to do with?

FRANK: Ships.

BETSY: Ships.

FRANK: Ships are the strongest things there are. A ship changes the world. Everything comes from ships. Look, when I was little, on the plantation, it was an island. You could always see the sea, always hear it, always smell it. The white men had brought us there in ships, back before I was born or before my mammy was born. When the slaves came, it was because the white men had brought them there in ships. I used to think, if us black people had a ship of our own we could get into it and sail away, back to where we came from or to some other place where the white men would never find us. It was ships, ships all the time, looking at them in the day, dreaming about them in the night. And soldiers kept coming to the island in ships, and other soldiers going away, and one day a ship brought some soldiers and one was Colonel Bathurst. I don't remember that, but I knew he must have come in a ship because soldiers always did. And when it came time for him to get on board the ship to go home, to come back to England, he took little Frank with him. So I wasn't a slave any more. A ship had changed that. But I was a servant. And it came to me that a ship could change that too.

BETSY: And did it?

FRANK: Look, Betsy, try to understand this. The ship changed everything all right. At first it changed it all to nightmare. I thought I must have died and gone to hell. Other times I reckoned the only thing left to do was jump over the side and drown myself. I thought the fishes would be kinder to me than the men who had the power over me. Even the sharks would.

BETSY: [*melting*] Oh, Frank.

FRANK: But I came through it. I didn't jump over the side. I lived and I sweated it out. I got to a position where they stopped picking on me, where they left me alone to do things my own way, and I had some friends who liked me for myself. I'd done it, I'd built a world for myself and I was living in it. I'd done it, Frank Barber, it was a world Frank Barber had made for Frank Barber to live in.

BETSY: So you had Frank, and it was.

FRANK: Then I started to look forward to the future. Maybe I'd be on a ship that'd go to Jamaica. We'd put into the harbour and we'd get a little shore leave. And there I'd be, little Frank the slave, I'd be walking around the waterfront and up the streets going up that hill, looking everybody in the face. And I used to dream I'd meet that overseer who used to whip my little back, out there in the hot sun, till the flies gathered round. And I'd stand right in front of him and I'd be wearing the uniform of a British Jack Tar. He wouldn't dare put a finger on me even if I was to spit right in his eye.

BETSY: I can see it all, Frank, all of it.

FRANK: And if I didn't meet that overseer I'd meet somebody just like him. And if I didn't go to Jamaica I'd go to some place just like Jamaica. Some place where blacks like me had to lie down and let the white people walk over them. Except when the black man was wearing a uniform that had been issued to him by the King of England. It was a different story then — when the King of England had said to the black man, 'Go out on the ocean and fight all my enemies — sink their ships and down them!'

[*Short pause.*]
And then the Doctor blew his bloody whistle and I had to come back here, to sweeping up and making beds, and this kitchen, and the old blind woman and that scavenger crab Levet!

BETSY: [*softly*] And me.

11. Wedding bells.

LEVET: Little black Frank, a married man! It's come at last.

ANNA WILLIAMS: I'm sure the Doctor is right — it'll make a man of him.

LEVET: And a good-looking wench too. She could 'a done better for herself.

ANNA WILLIAMS: It'll be the beginning of a new life for you, Frank.

[*Voices begin to chime in, wedding bells still in background.*]

BETSY: Frank, you must settle down.

LEVET: The best of everything.

ANNA WILLIAMS: The priceless gift of education.

LEVET: Too proud to get his hands dirty.

JOHNSON'S VOICE: Frank!

ANNA WILLIAMS: Betsy was the salvation of him.

LEVET: Parcels of stinking fish.

BETSY: You can be Betsy Barber's husband.

ANNA WILLIAMS: The Doctor knows what's best.

[*Sudden silence.*]

12. We hear the squalling of a newborn baby.

BETSY: What are we going to call him, Frank?

FRANK: Richard.

BETSY: Richard! Why Richard?

FRANK: I don't know what Colonel Bathurst's first name was. I never heard anyone call him by it. But Richard was the name he gave his son, and if it's good enough for Colonel Bathurst it's good enough for Frank Barber.

BETSY: I'm disappointed, Frank.

FRANK: What about?

BETSY: That isn't the name I expected you'd want to give him.

FRANK: Well, you asked me.

BETSY: Don't you want to know what name I expected, you big idiot?

FRANK: Well, what?

BETSY: Samuel, of course, Samuel!

FRANK: Oh — oh, that.

BETSY: Look, Frank, I don't often put my foot down and I know I said in church I'd love, honour and obey, and so I will, but I carried this baby for nine months and I've given birth to him and we're going to call him Samuel. We'll have lots more children and you can call the others anything you like, but this one, the first-born, is going to be Samuel.

FRANK: [*dejectedly*] So I'm going to be Dr Johnson's boy in that too.

BETSY: Are we going to have all that again? [*wheedling*] Frank, think what it'll mean to the Doctor. He's got no children of his own — little Sam'll be like a grandson to him.

FRANK: Betsy, the Doctor this, the Doctor that, but you've been good to me. I don't know what I owe the Doctor but I know what I owe to you, and if you want him called Sam we'll call him Sam.

BETSY: You're a good husband to me, Frank. I always knew you would be.

FRANK: It's what I want to be, anyway.

BETSY: Bend down and give me a kiss.

13. Footsteps. A burst of children's laughter.

LEVET: [*disgruntled*] Kids, kids, bowling hoops, playing marbles, it's not safe to walk along the pavements. And you can't dust 'em away 'cause half of 'em are Frank's.

ANNA WILLIAMS: In my opinion children's voices make a cheer-
     ful sound.
LEVET: That's because you've got nothing to do with your time.
     If you had work to get on with you'd find 'em what I do
     — a dratted nuisance.
          [*Another burst of laughter.*]

14. FRANK *is peeling potatoes in the kitchen.*

SAMUEL: Dad, why am I black?
FRANK: You're not very black. Your mother's white so you're
     only half black.
SAMUEL: But you're all black, aren't you, Dad?
FRANK: Yes.
SAMUEL: Why are you?
FRANK: 'Cause I come from the part of the world where the sun
     shines hot and it makes people dark.
SAMUEL: Like when you do potatoes in the oven?
FRANK: Yes, just like that. Potatoes in the oven.
SAMUEL: Is it nice there? I suppose it can't be, else you wouldn't
     have left and come here.
FRANK: It's nice enough, from what I remember, but it's a no-
     good place to live in for black people.
SAMUEL: Aren't they all black?
FRANK: No, some of them are white.
SAMUEL: Will the white ones go dark?
FRANK: If they stay there long enough I expect they'll go dark.
SAMUEL: If they stay till they're old.
FRANK: No, no, longer than that.
SAMUEL: If they stay till they're very old. Like Mr Levet.
FRANK: No, no. They'd go dark through the generations.
SAMUEL: What's a generation?
FRANK: When people have children and then the children have
     children and then the children have children.
SAMUEL: Am I a generation?
FRANK: Yes. You and your brothers and sisters.
SAMUEL: Shall we go white because we live here and not there?

FRANK: Not yourself. Your children might start going a bit more white. Specially if you all marry white people.

SAMUEL: Does marrying white people make black people go white?

FRANK: It makes their children go white a bit faster.

SAMUEL: Is that why you married mama?

FRANK: No, it isn't.

SAMUEL: Did she marry you because she wanted her children to be black?

FRANK: Look, we didn't care what colour our children were. We got married because we loved each other.

SAMUEL: If a green man married a pink lady what colour would their children be?

FRANK: Stop bothering me. There aren't any green men or pink ladies.

SAMUEL: There are tho'. I saw it written up over a tavern just near here. The Green Man, it was called. With a picture, and all.

FRANK: That's just a name.

SAMUEL: Why do they have the name if they don't have the thing?

FRANK: I don't know. Go away.

SAMUEL: Does the Doctor know?

FRANK: Don't you dare pester the Doctor.

SAMUEL: When you want to know something you ask the Doctor, don't you?

FRANK: Sometimes.

SAMUEL: Why not always?

FRANK: Look, I'm trying to peel these potatoes. If you ask me one more question, you can come and stand here and peel them yourself.

SAMUEL: I just remembered. I have to go out and play.

[*Footsteps recede. Others approach. They are* BETSY'*s.*]

BETSY: Are those potatoes ready?

FRANK: Betsy, you should find Sam something to do.

BETSY: He's only six. Let him play for a bit yet, he'll work long enough.

FRANK: Six! You know what I was doing when I was six?

BETSY: I should know. You talk about it enough.

FRANK: I don't talk about it. I never talk about it.

BETSY: Not to say talk about it, no. Not in just those words. But about three-quarters of the things you say, mean that.

FRANK: How d'you make that out?

BETSY: You've never got over being born a slave, have you, Frank? Every morning when you wake up you say to yourself: 'I'm Frank Barber, I'm black and I was born in slavery, and these white people have never stopped pushing me around, and I can't do what I like with my life.'

FRANK: I don't say that.

BETSY: You don't say it, but that's how you see things, isn't it? You even think the Doctor makes a slave of you.

FRANK: Are we going to have all that again? How I'm not grateful to the Doctor, how good the Doctor's been to us, how the Doctor this and the Doctor that?

BETSY: Frank, name one person in your life that you've really loved.

FRANK: You.

BETSY: That's nice of you and I love you too. But now give me another.

FRANK: Someone I love?

BETSY: Someone you've really loved in your life.

FRANK: Er...

BETSY: I'll save you racking your brains. There's only one person you've loved in your life. One man anyway. Colonel Bathurst.

FRANK: That was a long time ago.

BETSY: Time don't make no difference to those things, Frank.

FRANK: No. I suppose not.

15. Plantation bell: work song: voices in FRANK's *memory.*

BATHURST: What's your name, my boy?

FRANK: Frank, sir.

BATHURST: Frank what?

PLANTATION OWNER: Slaves don't have surnames, sir.
           [*Work-song again.*]

16. Footsteps. FRANK *is coming downstairs to* BETSY.

FRANK: I can't wake him.

BETSY: Who? The Doctor?

FRANK: No — Levet.

BETSY: You can't wake Levet?

FRANK: He's just lying there in his bed and when I touched his hand it felt very cold. I think he's dead, Betsy.

BETSY: But he was all right last night. He went out, I saw him.

FRANK: Well, come and see him now.

BETSY: All right, I'll come up.
           [*Sound of children playing and laughing. Window flying up.*]

FRANK: Quiet, you children, quiet! [*They cease.*] And Sammy, go and get your black coat and put it on. We have to observe mourning from now till the funeral.

SAMUEL: Whose funeral, Dad?

FRANK: Dr Levet's died.

SAMUEL: [*wonderingly*] Dr Levet? I didn't think he could die.

FRANK: Yes, lad, he was like old Father Time, standing in the corner watching us all, but he's gone.

SAMUEL: Father Time is gone.

FRANK: Get your black coat. And if you're going to play games, go a long way from the house where you can't be heard. This has to be a house of mourning.

SAMUEL: Are you mourning, Dad? Are you sorry about Dr Levet?

FRANK: Dr Johnson is, and that's what matters in this house.
           [*Footsteps descending stairs.*]

BETSY: Is he still sitting in his room?

FRANK: Yes, just sitting there.

BETSY: Doesn't he want anything?

FRANK: He'd let the fire go out. I had to re-light it. And I don't even think he noticed. He's just sitting there, staring in front of him.

BETSY: I didn't think Levet dying would be such a shock to him.

FRANK: I did. He always expected to go first.

BETSY: He's not quite alone. There's still Miss Williams.

FRANK: Yes, and she's not long for this world. She's very helpless. She was asking me today if we couldn't move in, you and I, and be under the same roof as her and the Doctor, instead of going home every night.

BETSY: What, and bring the children as well?

FRANK: What else?

BETSY: [*after a slight pause*] I don't like it, Frank. I know it's got to be done, but that doesn't make me like it. All through the years we've had our own little house just round the corner from the Doctor's, and now we've got to give it up and move into this... this house of the dead.

FRANK: It won't be a house of the dead any more, Betsy, when we move in with all the children.

BETSY: I know you're right and yet even that frightens me. We're caught between the young and the old. Caught between the growing and the dying.

FRANK: How d'you mean, caught? What's catching us?

BETSY: Don't you feel sometimes, Frank, as if we were on a narrow strip of land between two seas? In one sea, the tide's coming in very fast, it's rising and rising, big waves pouring in. The other sea's going out just as fast. So you and me have to keep moving over and moving over, with the children coming in like one sea and the old people going out like the other.

FRANK: [*resignedly*] Well, there's nothing we can do about it.

BETSY: That's why it frightens me.

JOHNSON'S VOICE: Frank!

FRANK: The Doctor. He's roused himself enough to want something, at any rate.

BETSY: Perhaps it isn't for himself. Perhaps it's Miss Williams wants something.

FRANK: Why doesn't she ring the bell, then?

BETSY: She's sinking, Frank, she may not have the strength to reach out and ring her bell.

VOICE OF ANNA WILLIAMS: My dark life is drawing to its end. So many years I have seen nothing. I have known his goodness, his love and protection, through sound only. I have communicated with him by talk and by pouring out of tea. My finger inside the cup: the touch of the hot liquid. And now I am going. Is it darkness I go towards, or light? Well, if it is darkness it will be nothing new to me. And if it is light... ah, if it is light...

17. Solemn, tolling bell.

FRANK: She's gone, then.

BETSY: Will you miss her?

FRANK: I dunno. I might. She goes back to the first time I ever saw this house. When you've known somebody that long... I even miss Levet; I never thought I would.
            [*Pause.*]

BETSY: Well, there's only one left to go.

FRANK: And when he goes, we all go.

BETSY: We'll still have our lives, Frank. And each other. And the children.

FRANK: Yes, the children, and they'll still want to eat when the Doctor dies and this house is sold off and we're on the street.

BETSY: I've thought about it, Frank, don't think I haven't.

FRANK: And what have you thought about it?

BETSY: Well, you'll have to look round for a new situation.

FRANK: That's easier said than done.

BETSY: Look, everything's easier said than done. And I'll take in washing.

FRANK: And bend over a tub and get your face red in the steam and all the curl taken out of your hair and your hands all crinkly.

BETSY: What are you talking about?

FRANK: Oh, just something you said the first time I ever talked to you.

BETSY: I remember... But oh, Frank, what can we do?

FRANK: We'll do something. We don't have to give up and starve.

BETSY: [*slowly, thoughtfully*] Doesn't it sometimes seem to you, when you look back, that it's been an easy life all these years? A carefree life?

FRANK: Compared with what's coming, yes.

BETSY: You've been under the Doctor's wing all these years. And now that wing's going to be taken away.

FRANK: Are you trying to tell me something new?

BETSY: It's just that... I've never heard you say you're grateful.

FRANK: I never have said it.

BETSY: But you should have done. You should have said it to him. He was your father, Frank, your father, and you didn't show any love to him.

FRANK: Well, if that's true, it only makes me the same as most sons have been, since the world began.

JOHNSON'S VOICE: [*feebly*] Frank!

FRANK: He's going down fast. His voice hardly reaches down here now.

BETSY: Well, it did reach, so go and see what he wants.

FRANK: All right. If you want something to do while I'm upstairs, this shirt needs mending. We've got to be careful with everything from now on.

BETSY: I've got plenty to do while you're upstairs.

[*His footsteps depart. She soliloquizes.*]

BETSY: Frank, Frank, the children are asleep, the old people are dead or dying, and there's just you and me left in the world. But then... you funny old black devil, ever since you made me fall in love with you, all that time ago, there only has been you and me in the world. Everybody else just... came and went.

18. While BETSY *waits downstairs, voices pick up the thread of the story.*

ANNA WILLIAMS: The Doctor says it'll make a man of him.

LEVET: It's worse than Bedlam where he's gone.

BETSY: You can be Betsy Barber's husband.

FRANK: I thought the fishes would be kinder to me.

ANNA WILLIAMS: The priceless gift of education.

LEVET: Propping up the railings in the middle of the morning.

19. FRANK's *hurrying feet come down the stairs.*

FRANK: Betsy! Betsy!

BETSY: I'm here, just where I was half an hour ago, mending the same shirt. You don't have to shout the place down.

FRANK: Yes, I do. I have to shout all over this house and all over London and all over the world. Everybody's going to hear what I've got to shout, yes, and the birds up in the sky and the fishes down in the sea.

BETSY: Can I hear what it is, or would that be too much?

FRANK: We're saved, Betsy. Everything's going to be all right. You needn't take in washing, I needn't knock on doors looking for a new job, the children'll have good food and good clothes.

BETSY: Why... What miracle has happened?

FRANK: The Doctor's made his will. He's had it witnessed by Mr Strahan and Mr Desmoulins. And guess who it's in favour of.

BETSY: Well, tell me, tell me, put it into words for me!

FRANK: 'My money and property, together with my books, plate and household furniture, to be applied, after paying my debts, to the use of Francis Barber... my man-servant, ...a negro...' [*He weeps.*]

BETSY: Did he say anything else?

FRANK: For a long time I couldn't speak, and he didn't say anything either. Then he said to me, 'When you get this inheritance, Frank,' he says, 'get out of London. There's

too many clever people here,' he says, 'they'll have your
money out of you. You've been a good boy, Frank, but
you're not clever. So get out of London.'

BETSY: Funny, that, when he's always said London's the finest
place in the world.

FRANK: The finest place for the likes of him, with brains and
strength. But dangerous for somebody who's not clever,
specially if they've got a bit of money they can be talked
out of. He's right, Betsy.

BETSY: Where shall we go?

FRANK: 'Well,' I said to him, 'Lichfield's the only place I know
well outside London, I've been there so many times with
you, I'll go to Lichfield.' That seemed to please him.
'Yes,' he says, 'you go and finish out your life in Lichfield
where I was born — that'll bring it round in a full circle,'
he says.

BETSY: You see — he does think of you as his son. That's how
he's always thought of you.

FRANK: I know, Betsy. I know... now.

BETSY: Thank God for the day you came into this house,
Frank.

FRANK: Miss Williams told me I was privileged. But even Miss
Williams didn't know the half of it.

BETSY: Did the Doctor say anything else?

FRANK: No. After he said that about Lichfield, and coming full
circle, he sent me downstairs again. You see, he's very
busy... dying.

20. Stafford Infirmary, January 1801. A bell tolls. FRANK's *enfeebled
voice: he is in his fever. Ghost voices of other characters.*

FRANK: Very busy dying... very busy dying.

LEVET: Take your time, lad. We all do it in our own way. I went
sudden, in my sleep. But then I always was lucky.

ANNA WILLIAMS: I shall comfort your wife, Frank. I shall be near
her and comfort her.

FRANK: But I want to do that! I want to be near her!

ANNA WILLIAMS: Oh, you will, you will.

CAPTAIN: You have your discharge, Barber, and you're going. Don't let me catch you aboard this ship in the morning.

SAMUEL: Dad, why am I black?

LEVET: Take your time, lad.

BETSY: There's someone to see you, Frank.

FRANK: Someone! There's everyone! The place is crowded. This kitchen hasn't got room for all the visitors. They all come to Gough Square — Frank has to let 'em in. Up the stairs, down the stairs, up the stairs, down the stairs. Haven't they got homes of their own?

BETSY: No, but this is somebody very special. Somebody you've always talked about. Well, he's come back, he's here to see you.

BATHURST: Frank, are you awake?

FRANK: Colonel Bathurst!

BATHURST: I'm going to sit down by your bed, Frank, and talk to you for a while.

FRANK: Just a minute, Colonel sir, I'll get out of bed, I'll fetch you anything you want. I think my clothes should be just here... my clothes... Colonel, somebody's taken Frank's clothes!

BATHURST: It doesn't matter about your clothes, Frank. Stay where you are for the moment. All I have to say is this.

FRANK: Can't I fetch you anything, Colonel? A drink? Your house-coat?

BATHURST: There's nothing I need, Frank. But you must listen to what I say now. Are you listening?

FRANK: Yes, Colonel.

BATHURST: You remember when you were a little fellow, you came with me on a ship. We made a long journey, didn't we, Frank?

FRANK: Yes, Colonel.

BATHURST: And we got to England, where you've lived your life. Well, now I've come to take you on another journey, to another life. It's a long way, but we'll get there, just as we got here all those years ago.

FRANK: When we get there, Colonel, will the Doctor be there?

BATHURST: Yes, Frank, the Doctor will be there.

FRANK: I'm ready then, Colonel. I'm ready any time.

BATHURST: Come then, Frank, come with me.

> [*The bell of Stafford Infirmary tolls, growing louder, then fading.*]

THE END

THE END